Sonia Soto

📖 CHERRY LAKE PRESS

Published in the United States of America by Cherry Lake Publishing
Ann Arbor, Michigan
www.cherrylakepublishing.com

Reading Adviser: Beth Walker Gambro, MS, Ed., Reading Consultant, Yorkville, IL
Illustrator: Leo Trinidad

Photo Credits: © Felix Lipov / Shutterstock, 5; © GM/Current Affairs / Alamy Stock Photo, 7, 9; © f11photo / Shutterstock, 11, 22; © ASSOCIATED PRESS, 13, 17, 19, 21; Souza / National Archives, 15, 23

Cherry Lake Press is an imprint of Cherry Lake Publishing Group

Library of Congress Cataloging-in-Publication Data

Names: Perez Mendoza, Brenda, author. | Trinidad, Leo, illustrator.
Title: Sonia Sotomayor / By Brenda Perez Mendoza ; illustrated by Leo Trinidad.
Description: Ann Arbor, MI : Cherry Lake Publishing, 2025. | Series: My itty-bitty bio | Audience: Grades K-1 | Summary: "Sonia Sotomayor rose to a seat on the highest court in the country. This early reader biography introduces young readers to her life and achievements in a simple, age-appropriate way. The My Itty-Bitty Bio series celebrates diversity, covering women and men from a range of backgrounds and professions who embody values that readers of all ages can aspire to"-- Provided by publisher.
Identifiers: LCCN 2024037646 | ISBN 9781668956236 (hardcover) | ISBN 9781668957080 (paperback) | ISBN 9781668957950 (ebook) | ISBN 9781668958827 (pdf)
Subjects: LCSH: Sotomayor, Sonia, 1954---Juvenile literature. | Hispanic American judges--Biography--Juvenile literature. | Women judges--United States--Biography--Juvenile literature. | Judges--United States--Biography--Juvenile literature. | United States. Supreme Court--Officials and employees--Biography--Juvenile literature.
Classification: LCC KF8745.S67 P47 2025 | DDC 347.73/2634 [B]--dc23/eng/20240816
LC record available at https://lccn.loc.gov/2024037646

Printed in the United States of America

table of contents

About the author: Brenda Perez Mendoza is an award-winning educator and the author of the Racial Justice in America: Latinx American series. She grew up in Cicero, Illinois, as a native language Spanish speaker. When she went to school, there wasn't enough support for students learning the English language. That is what drove her to become a K–12 ELL specialist and work with bilingual students. She works to advocate for all students, Latinx especially, to embrace their culture and celebrate who they are. Today, she lives in Chicago, Illinois, and is committed to providing students with culturally responsive practices and advocating for the whole child.

About the illustrator: Leo Trinidad is a NY Times bestselling comic book artist, illustrator, and animator from Costa Rica. For more than 12 years he's been creating content for children's books and TV shows. Leo created the first animated series ever produced in Central America, and founded Rocket Cartoons, one of the most successful animation studios in Latin America. He is also the 2018 winner of the Central American Graphic Novel contest.

my story

I was born in New York City in 1954. My family lived in the Bronx. My parents were Puerto Rican.

My father died when I was 9.

What is important to you?

I loved school. I loved to read most of all.

I worked hard in school.

9

I went to Princeton University. Then I went to Yale Law School.

I became a **lawyer**.

I later became a judge.
I still believed in education.
I **mentored** students.

I wanted kids from places like
the Bronx to succeed.

I was appointed to the **Supreme Court**. That was in 2009. I was the first **Hispanic** Supreme Court Justice.

I was the third woman to serve.

I believe in fairness. I believe in community. I believe in **equality**.

I believe in the rule of law.

What do you believe in?

In 2016, I was given the Hispanic Heritage Award for Leadership. To me, leadership means service.

I serve my country and my community.

Today, I still sit on the Supreme Court. I write books. I give talks. I want kids to know they can make a difference.

I want them to celebrate who they are.

What would you like to ask me?

1979

1950

Born
1954

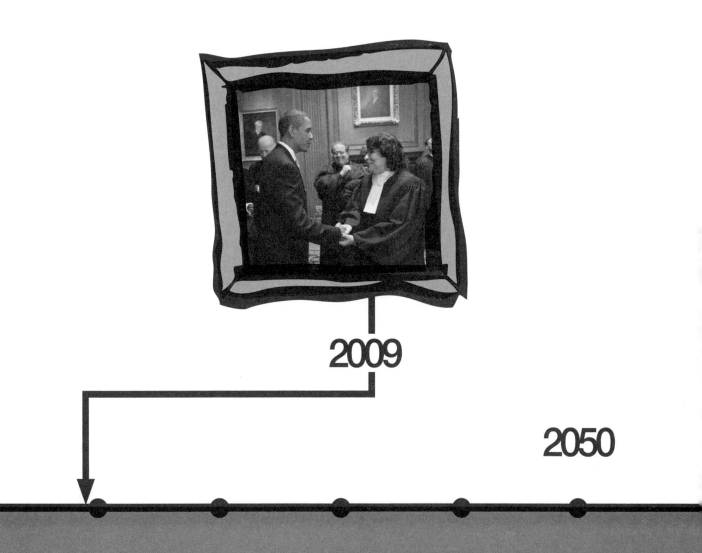

2009

2050

glossary

equality (ih-KWAH-luh-tee) the state of each person being equal to all others

Hispanic (hih-SPAA-nik) a Spanish-speaking person

lawyer (LOY-uhr) a person who works with the laws of a society

mentored (MEN-tord) taught and guided another person

Supreme Court (suh-PREEM KORT) the highest court in the United States

index

24